Comets, Asteroids and Meteorites

Written by
Cynthia Pratt Nicolson

Illustrated by
Bill Slavin

Kids Can Press

For my family

Acknowledgments

For their generous sharing of time and expertise, I would like to thank two astronomers,
Dr. Tom Gehrels of the University of Arizona and Dr. Colin Scarfe of the University of Victoria.
Their comments have contributed greatly to the scientific accuracy of this book. Of course,
any errors that may have slipped in are my responsibility.

I would also like to thank the staff at the Vancouver Public Library and teacher-librarian
David Gloag for their cheerful help with finding information on just about anything — from
activities about comets, to the name of an Alabama woman bruised by a meteorite in 1954.

As always, I appreciate the commitment to excellence shown by everyone at Kids Can Press.
My special thanks go to Laura Ellis for her thoughtful editing of this book, our first project
together. Finally, I would like to thank my family and friends for their never-ending support.

Text copyright © 1999 by Cynthia Pratt Nicolson
Illustrations copyright © 1999 by Bill Slavin

Kids Can Press acknowledges the financial support of the
Ontario Arts Council, the Canada Council for the Arts and
the Department of Cultural Heritage.

Published in Canada by
Kids Can Press Ltd.
29 Birch Avenue
Toronto, ON M4V 1E2

Published in the U.S. by
Kids Can Press Ltd.
85 River Rock Drive, Suite 202
Buffalo, NY 14207

Edited by Laura Ellis
Design by Marie Bartholomew and Esperança Melo

Photo Credits
All photos used courtesy of NASA
Printed in Hong Kong by Wing King Tong Co. Ltd.

CM 99   0 9 8 7 6 5 4 3 2 1
CM PA 99   0 9 8 7 6 5 4 3 2 1

Canadian Cataloguing in Publication Data

Nicolson, Cynthia Pratt
      Comets, asteroids and meteorites

(Starting with space)
ISBN 1-55074-578-6 (bound)   ISBN 1-55074-580-8 (pbk.)

1. Comets – Juvenile literature. 2. Asteroids – Juvenile literature.
3. Meteorites – Juvenile literature. I. Slavin, Bill. II. Melo,
Esperança. III. Title. IV. Series.

QB721.5.N52   1999   j523.5   C99-930310-4

Kids Can Press is a Nelvana company

Contents

Space rocks: Comets, asteroids and meteorites

Rocks that drop from the sky. Strange lights that flash and glow. Craters that dent the ground. Long ago, people observed these things with wonder and fear.
Today we know much more about comets, asteroids and meteorites. Here's what scientists tell us about these amazing — sometimes dangerous — space rocks.

What is a comet?

A comet is a ball of ice, gas and rocky dirt. It circles the Sun in a long, nearly oval path called an orbit. When a comet passes near the Sun, it develops a large, glowing head and a long tail. Bright comets can be seen easily from Earth.

If you see a word you don't know, look it up in the glossary on page 39.

What is an asteroid?

An asteroid is a chunk of rock or metal that orbits the Sun. Most asteroids travel in a zone between the orbits of Mars and Jupiter, but some cross Earth's path. Asteroids are difficult to spot. Through a telescope, they look like tiny stars.

What is a meteorite?

Asteroids often collide with one another, scattering broken pieces in space. When one of these rocky fragments lands on Earth, it is called a meteorite.

Comets: The space travelers

A hazy ball of light glows eerily in the night sky. Today we know it is a comet making its long journey around the Sun. Long ago, people were frightened by these ghostly visitors. They blamed comets for storms, earthquakes, diseases and death.

Comet Halley, one of the most famous comets, has fascinated people throughout history.

Comet tales

In 1665, thousands of people in London, England, died of a terrible disease. The next year, fire nearly destroyed the city. Because two comets had just appeared in the sky, many people were convinced a comet meant disaster.

In ancient China, a comet's bushy tail reminded people of a broom. They said the gods used the comet to sweep away evil.

Comet Halley was gleaming as William the Conqueror prepared to invade England in 1066. Later the same year, William defeated Harold II at the Battle of Hastings. "The comet made us lose," said Harold's men.

A bright comet came into view shortly after Roman emperor Julius Caesar was murdered. Some said the comet was Caesar's soul, returning to haunt his enemies. Caesar's grandnephew and heir, Octavian, said the comet meant Caesar was a god.

What are comets made of?

Comets are often called "dirty snowballs." That's because each comet has a core — called its nucleus — that is made of dust, ice and frozen gases.

Each time a comet approaches the Sun, its frozen nucleus heats up. Gases and dust escape and surround the nucleus in a huge cloud called a coma. The Sun's energy pushes some of the comet's gas and dust into one or more long wispy tails.

If you built a model comet with a pea for the nucleus, your comet's coma would be as big as a football field. And the end of its tail might be 100 km (62 mi.) away!

nucleus

coma

gas tail

dust tail

What do comets look like?

Most comets are too small and too far away to be seen from Earth. When a comet passes near the Sun, however, its glowing coma makes it look much bigger and brighter in the night sky.

A bright comet is an amazing sight. It glows like a huge, hazy star with a long, ghostly tail.

In 1997, Comet Hale-Bopp glowed brightly with reflected sunlight for several weeks. Hale-Bopp will return in about 2400 years.

TRY IT!
Track comets on the Internet

You'll need:
○ a computer with Internet access
○ permission from a parent or teacher

The Internet sparkles with images of comets. On the World Wide Web you will discover pictures of comets, information about famous comets such as Hale-Bopp and Hyakutake, and news about comets that are just coming into view.

Try these sites for comet news:
The Comet Observation Home Page
http://encke.jpl.nasa.gov/

NASA's Near-Live Comet Watching System
http://comet.hq.nasa.gov/

The Nine Planets – A Multimedia Tour of the Solar System (comets section)
http://www.seds.org/billa/tnp/

Each of these sites will lead you to others. You will find more information about comets — plus asteroids, meteorites, planets and stars. Enjoy your space tour!

Why do comets have tails?

Comets have two types of tails — gas tails and dust tails. Both types appear when a comet is near the Sun.

A gas tail usually points straight behind the comet. It forms when electrically charged particles from the Sun — the solar wind — blow on the comet's coma.

A dust tail often curves away from the comet's path. Escaping gases push dust off the head of the comet. Because the dust tail is made of solid particles, it has a different shape than the gas tail. Some comets have several dust tails and a gas tail, too.

The name "comet" comes from the Greek words *astēr komētēs*, which mean "long-haired star."

Why do comet tails always point away from the Sun?

Comets' tails are blown outward from the Sun by the solar wind. Because a comet's tail is not caused by the comet's motion, it can even travel in front of the comet.

Comet Challenge: Can you tell from a comet's photo which way the comet is going? (See page 39 for the answer.)

Where do comets come from?

Comets are leftover bits from the formation of the solar system. These icy objects cluster in at least two different places. Short-period comets — ones that orbit the Sun in less than 200 years — lie in the Kuiper belt. This ring of comets is just outside the orbits of Neptune and Pluto.

Other comets surround the whole solar system in a huge swarm. This sphere of comets is called the Oort cloud after its discoverer, Jan Oort. The outer limits of the Oort cloud are 1000 times farther away from the Sun than Neptune and Pluto.

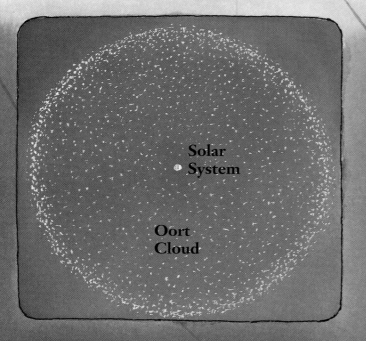

Solar System

Oort Cloud

What keeps a comet in orbit?

A comet is kept in its orbit by the Sun's strong pulling power, called gravity. Gravity also keeps Earth and the other planets circling the Sun.

Does a comet's orbit ever change?

A comet sometimes leaves its home in the Kuiper belt or the Oort cloud to travel closer to the Sun. Scientists think a comet in the Oort cloud might be pulled into its new orbit by a passing star. A comet in the Kuiper belt could be tugged by the gravity of a planet such as Neptune or Pluto.

Why do comets appear to stay still?

Comets are very far away. So even though they zoom quickly through space, we don't notice their motion. (Think of watching a plane in the sky — even though it is traveling fast, it seems to move slowly when it is far away.) To see a comet move, you need to watch its position over several nights.

How fast are comets?

Comets travel around the Sun at about 160 000 km/h (100 000 m.p.h.). This makes them some of the fastest things in the solar system.

Confusing as it may seem, a burned-out comet can become an asteroid.

How long do comets last?

Every time a comet passes the Sun, it loses ice, gas and dust from its nucleus. After about 500 passes, all that's left is a rocky lump.

Instead of shrinking gradually, a comet may be destroyed when it crashes into a planet or the Sun. Or the gravity of a passing planet may cause it to fly out of the solar system, never to be seen again.

Some comets have been around for hundreds or thousands of years. Comet Halley was recorded by Chinese astronomers in 240 B.C., so it is at least 2000 years old.

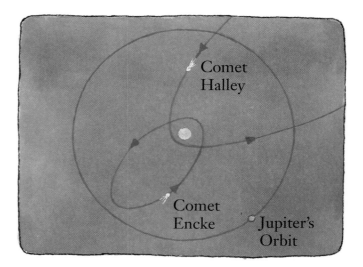

Comets with wide orbits usually last longer because they pass the Sun less often.

COMET FACT FILE

A comet's tail is spread so thin that a huge sports arena full of tail material would contain less matter than a teaspoon of ordinary air.

Comet West was so bright its head could be seen during the daytime in 1976.

Caroline Herschel (1750–1848) was the first woman to discover a comet. She also helped her brother William discover the planet Uranus.

The most frequent comet to orbit the Sun is Comet Encke. It passes around the Sun every 3.3 years.

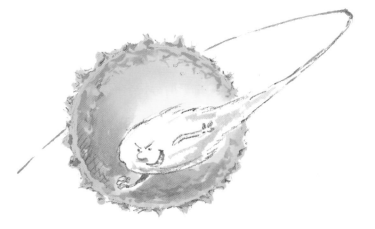

A comet's nucleus is a few kilometers (miles) across. Its coma is much wider — about 100 000 km (62 000 mi.). A comet's tail is amazingly long. It can stretch hundreds of millions of kilometers (miles).

Who made the first comet prediction?

In 1682, Edmond Halley watched a brilliant comet blaze in the sky over England. Then he figured out that two earlier comets had traced the same path. Each comet had followed the other by about 75 years.

Halley realized he was not studying three separate comets — just one that kept coming back. "It should return again around the year 1758," he wrote to a friend.

Halley's prediction came true in early 1759, and the comet was named after him. Comet Halley still reappears about every 75 years.

How do scientists predict comets?

Astronomers have used old records of comet sightings to identify about 180 comets with orbits shorter than 200 years. They also search the sky with powerful telescopes to find comets that are still a long way from Earth.

When a comet appears, scientists begin to measure its position. They need at least three different measurements to calculate the rest of its orbit.

But not all comets behave in ways that scientists expect. Sometimes an expected comet doesn't turn up, or it looks different from what was predicted. When Comet Halley returned in 1986, many people were disappointed because it wasn't very bright.

How are new comets discovered?

Comet hunters scan the night sky with telescopes, looking for anything unusual. Sometimes they find a fuzzy spot of light that isn't on the star maps. Right away, they contact other astronomers. Why the rush? If the new spot turns out to be a comet, it will be named after the one or two people who reported it first.

What happens when a comet hits a planet?

In July 1994, astronomers around the world pointed their telescopes at Jupiter. The giant planet was about to be hit by Comet Shoemaker-Levy 9, but no one could predict the size of the impact. On July 16, the comet plunged into Jupiter's foggy atmosphere. Some of the comet's 20 fragments produced huge gas geysers and explosions. Others left gigantic bruises. One dark splotch was wider than Earth. In a few days, Jupiter's rapid rotation turned the round scar into a dark band that circled the planet. The streak lasted for several months before it faded away.

These images, taken 2⅓ seconds apart, show a fragment of Comet Shoemaker-Levy 9 colliding with Jupiter.

Will a comet ever collide with Earth?

About 500 comets cross Earth's orbit as they travel around the Sun. Luckily, none of these comets appear to be on a collision course with Earth. Comets have bumped into Earth in the past and they will again, but the chances of a large impact happening in your lifetime are very small.

Bits of comet dust collide with Earth's atmosphere all the time. They usually burn up and can be seen as bright flashes of light called meteors, or shooting stars.

TRY IT!

See comet and asteroid craters on the Moon

Comets and asteroids have crashed into the planets — and even into our Moon — again and again. Check out the Moon and see the deep, wide craters left by these impacts.

> ### *You'll need:*
> - high-power binoculars
> - a clear night with a first or last quarter Moon (When the Moon is partially lit up, deep shadows help you see craters more clearly.)
> - a reclining lawn chair
> - the Moon map on this page
> - a flashlight covered with red tissue paper

1. Hold the binoculars steady by resting your elbows on the arms of the lawn chair. You may need to lay a board across the arms of the chair to make a comfortable support.

2. Focus the binoculars on the Moon's surface. Compare what you see with the Moon map. Hold the map so that it lines up with your view of the Moon.

3. The large dark areas are flatlands where lava flooded the Moon billions of years ago. They are called "maria" — seas — even though they contain no water. Look for craters in the areas between the maria.

4. Take a close look at the Tycho, Copernicus or Stevinus craters. Can you see the rays spreading from them? These rays are the patterns that formed when rock splashed out during a huge comet or asteroid impact.

Comet Challenge: Why do we see so many craters on the Moon and so few on Earth?
(See answer on page 39.)

First Quarter

Last Quarter

Mare Imbrium

Mare Serenitatis

Copernicus crater

Mare Tranquillitatis

Mare Nubium

Stevinus crater

Tycho crater

Asteroids: Mini-planets

Most of the time, asteroids float harmlessly in space. But once in a long while, an asteroid plunges toward Earth — with results that can be disastrous.

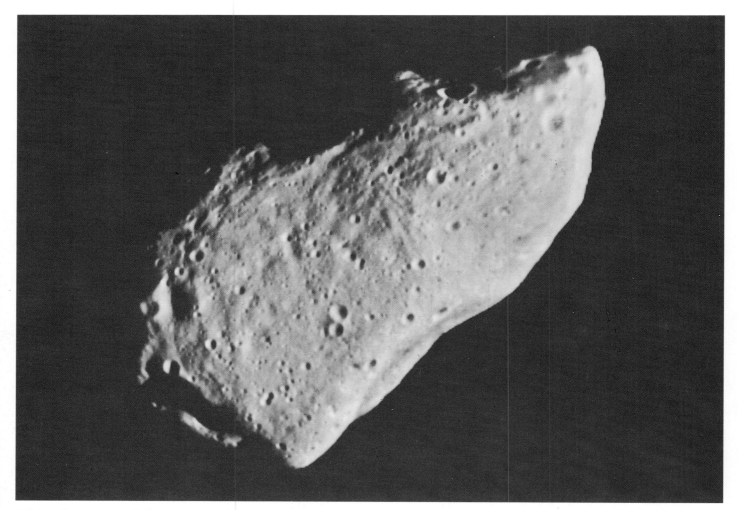

This close-up of the asteroid Gaspra was taken by the *Galileo* space probe. Gaspra is 19 km (12 mi.) long.

A deadly impact

A large asteroid — or possibly a comet — smashed into Earth 65 million years ago and destroyed the last of the dinosaurs.

How did it happen? The scene may have been like this: While *Triceratops* munched giant ferns, and *Tyrannosaurus rex* munched *Triceratops*, an asteroid hurtled toward Earth. It measured 12 km (7 mi.) across and dropped 300 times faster than a bullet shot from a gun.

The asteroid hit Earth with a crash that blasted a huge crater. Bits of burning rock flew off in all directions. Wherever the rocks landed, fires began.

Smoke from the fires and dust from the crash soon filled the air above the impact site. Within hours it blew around the whole planet and darkened the sky.

Without sunlight, most plants could not live. Animals had little to eat. Over time, all of the dinosaurs and many other animals became extinct. They had been killed by a visitor from outer space.

How did asteroids form?

About 4½ billion years ago, our solar system began from a huge, swirling cloud of gas and dust particles. The particles clumped together, forming the Sun and many smaller objects. Planets took shape when these small objects smashed together. After the planets formed, thousands of rocky bits were left over. Today we call them asteroids.

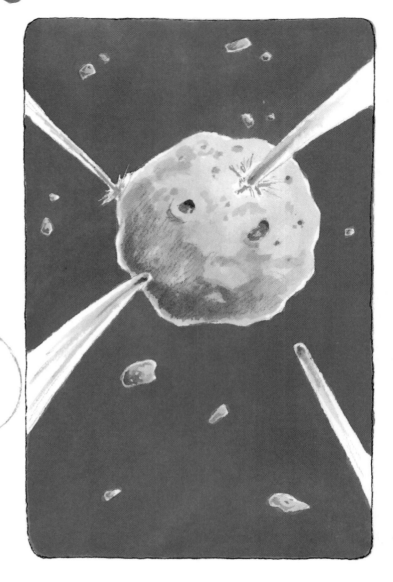

Their name means "starlike," but asteroids are nothing like stars. In fact, they are more like tiny planets. Astronomers call them "minor planets" and "planetesimals."

What are asteroids made of?

Most asteroids are made of rock. They are called stony asteroids. Some asteroids are made of iron, nickel and other metals. They are called iron asteroids. A few asteroids are made of a combination of rock and metal. They are known as the "stony-irons."

How is an asteroid different from a planet?

Asteroids are much smaller than planets and are shaped differently. Most asteroids do not have enough gravity to pull them into well-formed spheres. Instead of being shaped like a grapefruit, the average asteroid looks more like a lumpy baked potato.

TRY IT!
Make a reflector detector

An asteroid shines when sunlight bounces off it. But bigger asteroids are not always brighter than smaller ones. This activity shows you why.

You'll need:
- a medium-sized cardboard box
- black construction paper
- tape
- a mini-flashlight (one that takes AA batteries)
- a variety of old and new coins, including pennies, nickels, dimes and quarters

1. Lay the cardboard box on its side on a table so the opening is facing you.

2. Tape the black paper inside the box on the rear wall.

3. Place the flashlight inside the box, facing toward you and away from the black paper. Turn on the flashlight.

4. Hold one coin at a time in the flashlight's beam. Move the coin around until you see a spot of reflected light on the black paper.

5. Compare the light reflected by different coins. Can you find a dime that reflects more light than a quarter? Can you pick out a penny by its reflected light alone?

Like your coins, some asteroids reflect more light than others. Depending on its surface material, a small asteroid may be brighter than an asteroid twice its size. For example, Vesta, the fourth-largest asteroid, is brighter than Ceres, the largest asteroid of all.

How big are asteroids?

Ceres, the largest asteroid, would almost cover an area the size of Alaska. It measures 930 km (578 mi.) across. Next comes Pallas at about half that size. Pallas would cover Arizona. Altogether, astronomers have found about 200 asteroids wider than 100 km (62 mi.), but most are much smaller. Some are no bigger than a house.

Where are asteroids found?

Most asteroids circle the Sun in a series of rings called the main belt. This wide, flat band lies between the orbits of Mars and Jupiter. Unlike the asteroid-packed zone you might see in science-fiction movies, the main asteroid belt has plenty of empty space between asteroids. In fact, spacecraft traveling to Jupiter and beyond have passed through the asteroid belt unharmed.

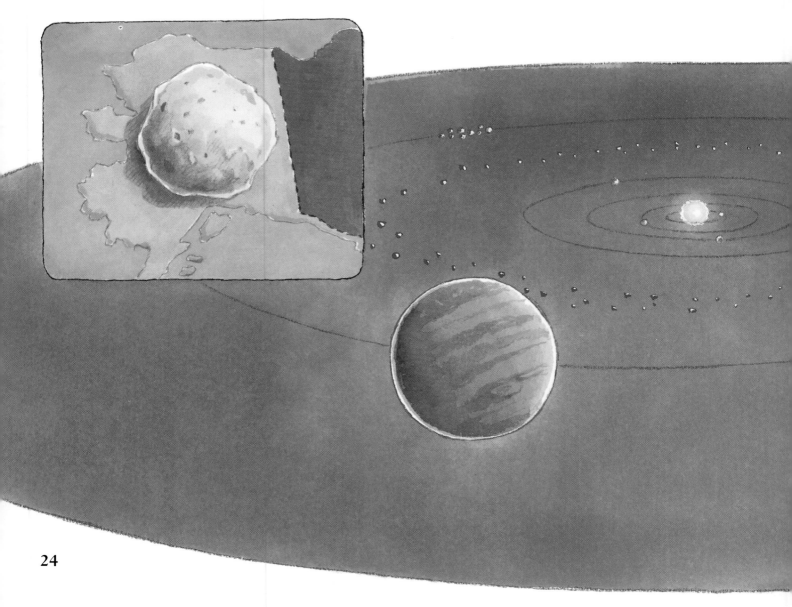

Do asteroids ever leave their orbits?

Asteroids sometimes crash into each other. These collisions can knock pieces out of the asteroid belt and into new orbits.

Some asteroids, called the Trojans, travel along the same path as Jupiter. Others, called the Amors, cross the orbit of Mars. Asteroids called the Apollos regularly cross the orbit of Earth.

The Moon shows the scars of countless comet and asteroid impacts.

How were asteroids discovered?

In 1800, astronomers knew that most planets seem to be spaced apart in an orderly way. They wondered why there was such a large gap between the orbits of Mars and Jupiter. Was there a missing planet?

In 1801, an Italian monk named Giuseppe Piazzi discovered a tiny object orbiting the Sun between Mars and Jupiter. He named it Ceres after the Roman goddess of grain.

But Ceres was too small to be a planet. Astronomers agreed to call it an asteroid because it looked like a small star through their telescopes. Within a few years, several more asteroids were found.

Does anything live on asteroids?

As far as we know, nothing lives on asteroids. However, some asteroids contain water, carbon and other compounds necessary for life. Life on Earth may have started when asteroids carried these compounds to our planet billions of years ago.

ASTEROID FACT FILE

If you could lump together all the asteroids in the asteroid belt, you would have a ball smaller than our Moon.

Vesta is the brightest of all the asteroids. If you know exactly where to look, it can be seen with binoculars.

Small asteroids often pass closer to Earth than the distance from Earth to the Moon.

About 5000 asteroids have been given official names and numbers. Asteroids 3350 to 3356 are named after the astronauts who died when the space shuttle *Challenger* exploded.

The planet Mars has two moons, Phobos and Deimos. These small, bumpy moons may be asteroids that have been captured by the gravity of Mars.

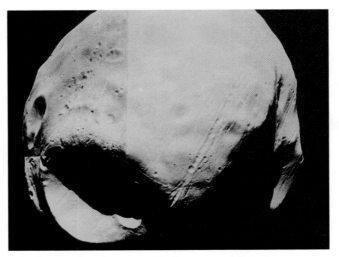

Phobos, the larger of the two Martian moons, is about 22 km (14 mi.) across.

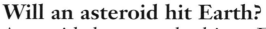

How do scientists study asteroids?

Even through telescopes, asteroids look like tiny dots of light. Still, astronomers are able to figure out what asteroids are made of by analyzing their reflected light.

While on its way to Jupiter in 1991, the *Galileo* space probe took photos of the asteroid Gaspra. These very first asteroid close-ups showed a rocky lump covered with craters. *Galileo* also sent back portraits of the asteroid Ida. Scientists were surprised by these snapshots. Ida has its own mini-moon!

The Near-Earth Asteroid Rendezvous (NEAR) mission is designed to approach the asteroid Eros in 1999 and send back plenty of new information.

Will an asteroid hit Earth?

Asteroids have crashed into Earth in the past and will hit our planet in the future. A few astronomers are studying near-Earth asteroids so they can predict the next big impact.

In March 1998, astronomers announced that an enormous asteroid might collide with Earth in 2028. Fortunately, the astronomers changed their prediction a few days later. Based on new data, they decided that the asteroid will pass Earth at a safe distance. Phew!

If an asteroid is detected heading for Earth, rockets and explosives may be used to push it away from our planet.

The asteroid Ida has its own mini-moon.

TRY IT!
Hard-hitting asteroids

Imagine two same-sized asteroids zipping toward Earth at the same speed. Which would hit with greater force — the one made of stone or the one made of metal? See for yourself in this activity.

You'll need:
○ a stone about half the size of a tennis ball
○ about 200 pennies
○ a measuring cup
○ water
○ two small yogurt containers

Step one: Match volumes of stone and metal

1. Place the stone in the measuring cup. Pour in enough water to reach the 250 mL (1 c.) mark.

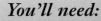

2. Carefully remove the stone from the cup. Notice how much the water level drops. The difference in level shows the volume of the missing stone.

3. Add enough pennies to replace the stone's volume. Stop when the water again reaches the 250 mL (1 c.) mark.

4. Drain the water. Pour the pennies into one yogurt container and place the stone in the other. Like two same-sized asteroids, your containers now hold matching volumes of stone and metal.

Step two: Compare the mass

Hold the container with the stone in one hand. Pick up the container with the pennies in your other hand. Which container is heavier?

Like your samples, a metal asteroid is heavier — and has more mass — than a stone asteroid the same size. In a head-on collision with Earth, the metal asteroid would produce a greater crash.

Meteorites: Stones from the sky

Every day, rocky invaders from outer space crash through Earth's atmosphere. The smaller ones burn up, leaving fiery trails of light called meteors. Larger pieces — meteorites — crash onto the ground. For centuries, people have been scared and excited about these rocks from space.

About 40 000 years ago, a house-sized iron meteorite slammed into the Arizona desert and left a huge hole called Meteor Crater. The crater floor is so large, it could hold 20 football fields.

Stories from the past

In many parts of Europe, people used to say that a meteor meant someone had died.

Native people of northern California said meteors were the souls of their leaders traveling to life after death.

In many parts of the world, people say you should make a wish when you see a meteor.

Ancient Egyptians did not know how to get iron from the ground. The only iron they had came from meteorites. People gave a special name to the rare metal they used for tools and weapons. They called it "stone of heaven."

The ancient Greeks placed an especially large meteorite in a sacred temple. They said it was the goddess Artemis, who had fallen from the sky.

Old German stories told of meteorites containing many strange things.  Some meteorites carried messages from the dead; others held ham, rotten cheese, silver, gold and money.

What is the difference between a meteoroid, a meteor and a meteorite?

A meteoroid is a small chunk of space debris left behind by a passing comet or asteroid.

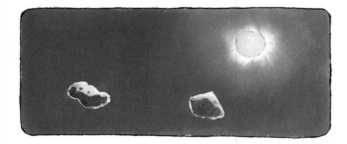

A meteor is the streak of light you see when a meteoroid burns up as it falls through Earth's atmosphere.

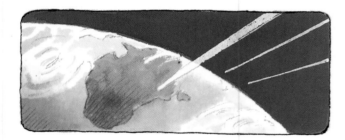

A meteorite is a meteoroid that survives its fall through the atmosphere and lands on Earth's surface.

Why are meteors so bright?

When a small meteoroid speeds into Earth's atmosphere, it may be traveling faster than a bullet from a gun. The air ahead of it quickly becomes so squished and heated that it glows. For a second or two, a meteor flashes across the sky. Incredible as it seems, some of the brightest meteors are produced by meteoroids no bigger than a grape.

Meteors are sometimes called "shooting stars," or "falling stars," even though they aren't stars at all.

What are meteorites made of?

Meteorites are made of metal or rock, or a combination of the two materials. Most meteorites are pieces of asteroids that break off when two asteroids collide.

The rock in an asteroid-type meteorite is as old as the solar system. If a meteorite is made of younger rock, scientists know it was probably thrown off the Moon or Mars during a major collision with an asteroid or comet.

Tiny meteorites, called micro-meteorites, float down to Earth as dust. Because they are so light, they don't travel fast enough to burn up in the atmosphere. Most of them come from the tail of a passing comet. Every year, 40 000 tonnes (39 400 tn.) of micro-meteorite material lands on Earth.

Meteorites that are spotted as they crash down are called "falls." Meteorites found on the ground are called "finds."

On October 9, 1992, Michelle Knapp heard a crash outside her home in Peekskill, New York. She discovered that her car had been hit by a football-sized meteorite.

What are meteor showers?

Meteor showers are displays of many meteors in one night. They happen when Earth passes through the dust trail left behind by a comet. Earth crosses several comet trails each year as it orbits around the Sun, so famous meteor showers are seen at the same time year after year.

What is a fireball?

A fireball is an extra-bright meteor produced when a large meteoroid plunges toward Earth. Some fireballs are so bright that they can be seen during the daytime. They are often accompanied by a series of loud bangs or thundering sounds. Some even explode in the sky.

A meteor shower won't get you clean. But it will give you a chance to see dozens of meteors in one night.

In 1908, a huge fireball exploded over a remote part of Siberia. People over 900 km (600 mi.) away heard the boom. It flattened trees for 32 km (20 mi.) around. The explosion was much greater than the 1980 eruption of the Mount St. Helens volcano.

TRY IT!

Watch a meteor shower

You'll need:
- a calendar that shows the Moon's phases
- a clear night with no full Moon
- a place with a wide-open view of the sky
- warm clothes
- an adult's permission to stay up really late

Meteor showers happen when Earth passes through dust left behind by a comet. Several showers can be seen regularly year after year. They are named after the constellations they appear to come from.

Here are names and dates* of the best meteor showers:

Quadrantids	January 3
Eta Aquarids	May 6
Perseids	August 12
Orionids	October 21
Leonids	November 16
Geminids	December 13

*You also might see meteor showers on the nights just before and after these dates.

1. Check out the meteor shower dates on your calendar. Look for showers that will happen when there is a new or crescent Moon. Plan to do some sky watching on those nights.

2. Go out as late as possible. The Geminid shower can be seen around 10 P.M., but most meteor showers are better after midnight, when your side of Earth is heading directly into the comet dust trail.

3. Avoid bright lights so your eyes will get used to the dark. If the weather is warm enough, lie down on a lawn chair or blanket for a more comfortable view.

4. Patiently scan the sky. You are watching for bright streaks of light that last about one second. On a dark, clear night you might see a meteor every minute or two. If you are near city lights or if the Moon is bright, meteors will be harder to see.

What happens when a meteorite hits Earth?

Tiny micro-meteorites fall to Earth all the time and we don't even notice them. Larger chunks of rock may land in the ocean or desert and never be observed. But sometimes a meteorite landing can't be ignored. Mrs. Elizabeth Hodges was badly bruised when a meteorite crashed through the roof of her Alabama home in 1954. Mrs. Hodges is the only person known to have been hit by a meteorite.

METEORITE FACT FILE

The largest meteorite in the world fell in southwestern Africa. Its estimated weight is over 50 tonnes (50 tn.).

A dog was killed by a meteorite that fell in Egypt in 1911. Scientists figured out that the rock had come all the way from Mars.

On April 26, 1803, thousands of small meteorites rained down on a town near Paris, France.

NASA scientists are studying a meteorite that formed on Mars and landed in Antarctica. The meteorite might hold microscopic fossils. Scientists are asking, "Was there once life on Mars?"

TRY IT!
Create some craters

Watch what happens when a meteorite strikes the ground. This activity can be messy, so ask an adult's permission before you begin.

You'll need:
- a large plastic bucket
- 500 mL (2 c.) flour
- 50 mL (¼ c.) cocoa powder
- a sifter
- an old newspaper
- three marbles

1. Spread the flour in the bottom of the bucket. Make it as smooth as possible.

2. Sift the cocoa to cover the surface of the flour.

3. Spread the newspapers on the floor and place the bucket on top of them.

4. Drop the marbles one at a time into the bucket.

5. Carefully remove the marbles and inspect your craters.

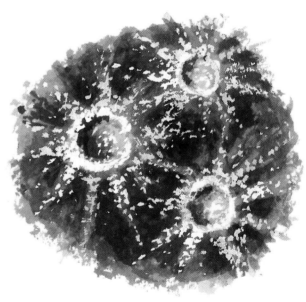

When a large meteorite hits Earth or the Moon, it splatters rock in all directions. The crater it produces often has a raised rim. Can you see these features in your craters?

Why study comets, asteroids and meteorites?

Although they come from outer space, comets, asteroids and meteorites can help us understand our world. Scientists are trying to answer many questions. Did comets bring water to our planet? How often have asteroids collided with Earth? Does a meteorite from Mars tell about ancient life on that planet?

Asteroids could be useful as refueling stations for space travelers, or as mines for precious minerals. By tracking comets and asteroids, we might be able to save ourselves from a disastrous collision.

We have learned many things about comets, asteroids and meteorites, but many more questions remain unanswered. Astronomers will continue their quest to learn more about these fascinating space rocks.

Glossary

asteroid: a rocky object orbiting the Sun

astronomer: someone who studies stars, planets and other objects in space

atmosphere: a layer of gases surrounding a planet

binoculars: an instrument that helps you see faraway objects more clearly

coma: a huge cloud of gas and dust surrounding the nucleus of a comet

comet: a ball of ice and dust that orbits the Sun

crater: a round hole made by a collision with a meteorite, asteroid or comet, or by the collapse of a volcano

fireball: an extra-bright and long-lasting meteor

gas: a form of matter made up of tiny particles that are not connected to one another and so can move freely in space. Air is made up of gases.

geyser: gas or liquid spurting up from the surface of a planet or moon

gravity: an invisible pulling force that pulls all objects in the universe toward one another

mass: the amount of matter in an object

meteor: the flash of light produced by a piece of rock or dust falling through Earth's atmosphere

meteorite: a space rock that has landed on Earth

meteoroid: a piece of dust or rock in space

micro-meteorite: a tiny space particle that floats down to Earth's surface

moon: a small body that circles a planet or asteroid

nucleus: the central core of a comet

orbit: a path around the Sun. Planets, comets and asteroids all have orbits.

planet: a large object that orbits a star and does not make its own light. Earth is a planet that circles a star called the Sun.

solar system: the Sun, its planets and their moons, plus smaller orbiting bodies such as asteroids and comets

solar wind: charged particles streaming away from the Sun

space probe: a robot-like spacecraft with no human crew

telescope: an instrument that makes very faraway objects seem nearer. Telescopes are often used to look at comets and asteroids.

Answers

Page 11: No, you can't tell from a photo which way a comet is going. The comet's tail always points away from the Sun, so it doesn't always travel behind the comet.

Page 19: Craters on Earth are worn away by wind, rain and snow. Because the Moon has no weather, its craters last for millions of years.

Index